S

on

RCPsych Publications/St George's, University of London
LONDON

4

6

9

11

29

35

36

The following words are provided for readers or carers who want a ready-made story rather than tell their own.

1. Polly points at a man outside. She looks upset.

2. They call the police. Frank helps her.

3. Frank is talking to a police officer on the phone. Polly looks worried.

4. The police officer comes to her home. He's come to talk about what happened. Polly tells him that the man hurt her.

5. The police officer explains about going to court. He says people who are victims can tell the court what happened. He tells Polly about the **special measures** she can choose to help her if she goes to court. For example, she can ask the judge and other people in court to take off their wigs; she can sit in the witness box behind a screen so she cannot see the man who hurt her; she can be interviewed by the policeman on a video.

6. The police officer is introducing the lady from the court to Polly and Frank.

7. She explains her job to them. She tells them she is an intermediary. She will help Polly understand questions she is asked. She will help her to speak up and tell her story. She won't think up answers for Polly but she can speak Polly's answers for her. She can also ask for questions to be put in a different way if Polly finds them difficult to understand.

8. Polly tells the policeman and the intermediary which **special measures** she wants – what would be good for her.

9. Polly and Frank go to the police station. The officer shows them the room where Polly's evidence will be video-taped. The intermediary is there as well.

10. The intermediary sits in the interview room. The camera is there. The policeman shows Polly and Frank the control room next door. They can see the intermediary on the television screen.

11. The policeman asks Polly some questions. She doesn't understand. The intermediary helps her. Polly tells them about the man who hurt her. Polly and the intermediary are on the television screen.

12. They tell Polly and Frank that the man has been arrested. He has been charged with a criminal offence.

13. The police officer is talking to a woman at Victim Support.

14. The woman from Victim Support comes to Polly's house. She has an identity card so that Polly knows who she is. They look at this book together.

15. Polly is crying. She is upset. She remembers what she went through. This book helps her to think about it.

16. Polly and the Victim Support worker talk about going to court.

17.   Polly and Frank visit the court. The intermediary is with them.

18.   The court usher shows them round.

19.   Polly wants to know what happens in court. The court usher tells her about the screen which she can stand behind. She will be able to see the judge, the barristers, other people working in the courtroom and the jury. She will *not* see the man who hurt her.

20.   The court usher tells Polly about the oath. This is when she promises that everything she says in court will be true.

21.   They leave the courthouse and say goodbye to each other.

22.   Polly is at home. She feels upset and worried.

23.   The Victim Support lady comes again. They talk about the man who hurt Polly.

24.   Polly and Frank read this book together. Now they know what will happen next.

25.   Polly looks at the calendar. It shows the date of the court case.

26.   Now they go back to court again. The intermediary goes too.

27.   They are waiting to go into court.

28.   The intermediary shows Polly where to go. They go behind the screen.

29.   Polly can see the judge, the people working in court and the jury. She cannot see the man who hurt her.

30.   The barristers take their wigs off.

31. Polly takes the oath. She says she will tell the true story. She will tell the court what happened.

32. Everyone is watching the video of Polly's interview with the police officer.

33. The prosecuting barrister asks Polly questions. He is trying to show that Polly is telling the truth and that the man did hurt Polly.

34. The defence barrister asks Polly questions. She is trying to defend the man and show that he did not hurt Polly.

35. Polly can't understand the questions. The intermediary speaks to the judge.

36. The judge says 'stop' to the barrister. Polly and the intermediary look pleased that the judge listens to them.

37. At the end of the questions they leave the courtroom. Polly can go home now.

38. Polly says 'I'm glad that's all over'. What happened feels a long time ago.

39. Polly sits quietly on a bench. She enjoys some time for herself. Her dog is with her.

Supporting Victims

If you are reading this book or have asked someone to read it to you – well done! It is brave and important to think about things like this. Perhaps you, or a friend of yours, are thinking about going to the police or court or you want to know what happens when people report a crime.

If someone hurts you by stealing your property, hitting you or having sex with you against your wishes, it is a crime. It hurts you and it is against the law. It is the job of the police to try and protect you.

If the police think you need help talking to them they can call an intermediary to listen and help. You can hear about special measures that will make you feel safer. For example, the court usher can show you a screen you can stand behind so you don't have to see the person who hurt you even though you can see the other people in the court.

The police can also call on Victim Support to visit you to listen to your worries and fears. Talking about what happened can be frightening and upsetting. Will it just make you remember all the bad things or will it offer you a chance to move on? Some people feel shy, or cry or cannot sleep, have nightmares and run to the toilet all the time. Others feel angry and violent.

Inside the court you get help from an intermediary who makes sure you understand what people are saying to you. She can tell the judge if you are finding it too hard.

There will also be a barrister on your side asking you questions. That is usually easier as the barrister knows your case and wants to help. Everybody has a barrister to help them, even the person who hurt you. Sometimes the other person's barrister asks questions too fast or loud or can say things that are not right. The intermediary can help you here.

Not every bad thing that happens to you can be proved in court. Sometimes the only person who knows what really happened is the person who hurt you and they don't want to tell the truth.

After the court is over there can be many different feelings. People can feel frightened, bad, sad, disappointed. Some feel bad if the person who hurt them goes to prison. Others feel bad because their abuser is still free. One woman, whose abuser was sent to prison, did not feel happy. She was worried the judge would know she had stolen a bar of chocolate when she was only a little girl! Courts are about truth and that often makes people think of little things they did wrong a long time ago even when they are in court as the victim. But for many, the most important thing is that they have a voice and are believed and listened to. Having a police officer, an intermediary, Victim Support and a judge all listen to you shows how powerful your voice can be.

Special measures

In the past, vulnerable witnesses have found it difficult and stressful to tell a court what has happened to them. In order to help them, in 1999 the Government passed the Youth Justice and Criminal Evidence Act. This is an Act of Parliament. It is the law. It provides special measures to help vulnerable and intimidated witnesses give their best evidence in court.

People who are considered to be vulnerable witnesses are those:

- under 17 years
- with a mental disorder or learning and developmental disabilities
- with a physical disorder
- with a physical disability (this includes deafness).

People who are frightened or distressed about giving their evidence are called intimidated witnesses.

In this book the police officer helps Polly to choose the special measures that could help her give her best evidence. He then tells the court what she needs. The court decides which special measures Polly uses. The court must explain why if it will not allow the use of a special measure.

Special measures are:

- using an intermediary to help the witness understand questions and to help the court understand the witness's answers
- live television link between the courtroom and another room where the witness gives evidence
- people in the court taking off their wigs and gowns

- screens used around the witness box so that the witness does not see the defendant
- the video recording of the witness's statement to the police – this is shown to the court.

Aids to communication can also be used to support witnesses in police interviews and in court. Aids include pencil and paper, pictures, symbol systems and signing.

Sometimes, members of the public are asked to leave the courtroom when the witness gives evidence. This measure can only be used in cases of sexual offences or when someone has tried, or might try, to frighten the witness.

Intermediary

The intermediary helps witnesses when they speak to the police and when they answer questions in court.

If the witness does not understand a question, the intermediary can ask for the question to be made simpler. If the witness's answers are hard to understand, the intermediary tells the court what the witness said.

If the witness needs a break, the intermediary asks the court.

Intermediaries are independent and do not ask their own questions or put forward their own views in court. They are not police, lawyers, appropriate adults or supporters. Their duty is to the court.

Live television link

A live television link means the witness can give evidence from outside the courtroom. The witness can sit in a private room away from the courtroom and give their evidence (tell their story) and answer questions through a live television link to the courtroom. The witness will be able to see and hear the person speaking in the courtroom and those in the courtroom can see and hear the witness on a television screen. The court usher sits with the witness in the television link room. The intermediary and/or a supporter may sit with the witness as well.

The video-recorded interview

When the witness tells the police what they know, it is recorded on a video-tape. The video will be shown in the courtroom at the time of the trial.

The video can be used as the first part of the witness's evidence in court. If some things are not clear in the video, the lawyers can ask the witness questions. A television link might be used for this.

Taking wigs off

The judge and lawyers can be asked to take off their wigs and gowns. Some witnesses prefer to see these people without the wigs and gowns. Other witnesses want them to keep them on.

Screen used around the witness box

Screens can be placed around the witness box. This way the witness does not see, and cannot be seen by, the person who is accused of doing the crime.

Evidence in private

The court can be cleared of most people, but legal representatives and some other people must be allowed to stay.

Some people you will see in court

In this book the crime is dealt with in the Crown Court. If the defendant says they did not commit the crime, there has to be a trial. In a Crown Court trial the judge is in charge. The jury decides if they think the defendant did the crime. Here are some of the people you will see in the Crown Court.

Judge

The judge is in charge of what happens in the court. He or she will make sure that everyone follows the rules of the court. The judge tries to make sure that everything is fair.

Barristers

The defence barrister's job is to help the defendant by telling the court what they say happened. The prosecuting barrister tells the court about how the defendant might have done the crime.

Defendant

The defendant (the accused) is the person who may have done the crime (broken the law).

Witness

The witness tells the court about something that happened. There may be more than one witness. A witness must always tell the truth. No one can hurt you for telling the truth.

Jury

These are twelve men and women who listen carefully to what everyone says in court. The jury must decide if the defendant did the crime.

Police officer

Police officers try to make sure that people are kept safe from crime. If a crime has been committed, the police will investigate the crime. They talk to all the people that might know something about what

happened. In court a security officer or prison officer makes sure that the defendant cannot speak to or go near any witnesses in court.

Court usher

The court usher tells witnes-ses when it is their turn to be a witness. They will show witnesses where to wait and where to go to give their evidence.

Some words you might hear in court

Accused   The person charged with breaking the law (also called the defendant).

Guilty   Someone is called guilty if the jury decides that they did the crime.

Not guilty   Someone is not guilty if the jury is not sure that the person did the crime. This does not mean that the jury did not believe the witness.

Judgment   The final decision of a court (also called the verdict).

Where to find help in England and Wales

Victim Support   **Support line: 0845 30 30 900**

Victim Support is the national service for crime victims, witnesses, their families and friends. A range of services is offered by Victim Support, whether or not a crime has been reported. Victim Support provides information, practical help and emotional support to people who have experienced a crime, and to their families and friends. After a crime has been committed, a Victim Support volunteer can visit the victim at home to offer support and someone to talk to in confidence about the crime.

All criminal courts in England and Wales now have a **Witness Service**, managed by Victim Support. Trained personnel help victims, witnesses and their families and friends at court by showing them round the court before the hearing, supporting them on the day, giving information about court procedures, and arranging further help after court. Where an intermediary is appointed, the Witness Service can assist the intermediary by explaining court procedures. The intermediary can assist the Witness Service to communicate with the witness.

For information about how to contact your local Victim Support or Witness Service use the support line given above. This national telephone helpline can also be used by people who want to talk anonymously about their experiences.

VOICE UK   **Helpline: 0845 122 8695**

VOICE UK is a national charity which tries to get justice for vulnerable people who have experienced crime or abuse. The helpline gives support and advice to vulnerable people who have experienced crime or abuse, their families, carers and professional workers.

VOICE UK has a caseworker who supports vulnerable people who have been sexually assaulted or abused. The caseworker can do this, both over the phone and face to face. The caseworker can offer ongoing support through the criminal justice system for vulnerable victims of sexual assault, by giving:

- help to vulnerable victims to understand what their rights are as witnesses
- emotional support to victims who have been sexually assaulted or abused
- support to victims at interviews and meetings
- help to vulnerable victims to make complaints, or to fill out forms to do with their case
- help to victims to be clearer about what the next steps might be to get what they want.

Call the VOICE UK helpline to speak to a caseworker.

Respond   Helpline: 0808 808 0700

Respond is a national charity which gives emotional support, advice and counselling to people with learning disabilities, who are either victims or perpetrators of sexual abuse. Support is also available to their carers. Respond's helpline is free for all ages, for support, counselling and advice.

Rape Crisis (England and Wales)

PO Box 254   Email: info@rapecrisis.org.uk
Hanley, Stoke-on-Trent
ST1 4RE

Rape Crisis is a national organisation which champions the needs of women and girls who have experienced sexual violence (either recently or in the past). It also coordinates the network of affiliated local rape crisis centres. To receive information about their activities or to find your nearest service, contact or write to them at the contact details given above.

Useful information

Together Against Abuse (free). This booklet helps families prevent abuse of people with learning disabilities in residential and day services.

Assert Yourself (video and book) (£25 + VAT). This book and training video, which is performed by actors with learning disabilities, helps people to be more assertive.

Stop! No More Abuse (2nd edn) (2003) (£5.00 per copy). This book is for people with learning disabilities to read alone or with a supporter. It helps people recognise the various kinds of abuse adults with learning disabilities may encounter in their daily life. The book encourages people to speak out about abuse.

Easy Read Guide to the Police (£1 per copy). *Easy Read Guide about Special Measures* (£1 per copy).

All the above are published by VOICE UK. Copies can be obtained from their website http://www.voiceuk.org.uk

The Survivor's Guide To Recovery from Rape or Sexual Abuse (R. Kelly & F. Maxted) (2005) (£15.99). Features a collection of unique illustrations portraying the stories of survivors. Offers helpful and friendly advice that can be used in everyday situations. Available from RoSA, PO Box 151, Rugby CV21 3WR and http://www.survivorguide.co.uk

What's My Story? (2006) (free). A guide to using intermediaries to help vulnerable witnesses. Included are two DVDs, one for vulnerable victims 'Sally Can Dance' and another for professionals 'A Voice for Vulnerable Witnesses'. Published by the Office of Criminal Justice Reform. To obtain a copy email intermediaries@cjs.gsi.gov.uk

Protecting You from Sexual Abuse (2005) (free). Home Office Crime Reduction team. A booklet about sexual abuse and the law for people with learning disabilities. For a copy telephone 020 7035 1700.

Some other titles in the Books Beyond Words series

Jenny Speaks Out (2nd new edition) (2005) This book may enable a person with learning disabilities to open up about their experience of sexual abuse.

I Can Get Through It (1998) shows how a woman is helped to get through the experience of being abused with the help of a counsellor or therapist.

Mugged (2002). When a young man is mugged he is helped by speedy police action, victim support and back-up of family and friends.

Log on to http://www.rcpsych.ac.uk/bbw for full details of all the titles available in the Books Beyond Words series.